DIG AND DISCOVER
PYRITE

by Nancy Dickmann

T0034192

CAPSTONE PRESS
a capstone imprint

Published by Capstone Press, an imprint of Capstone
1710 Roe Crest Drive, North Mankato, Minnesota 56003
capstonepub.com

Library of Congress Cataloging-in-Publication Data is available on the Library of
Congress website
ISBN: 9781666342628 (hardcover)
ISBN: 9781666342642 (paperback)
ISBN: 9781666342659 (ebook PDF)

Summary: Pyrite is also called fool's gold. Uncover how this golden mineral forms
and where you can find it.

All internet sites appearing in back matter were available and accurate when this
book was sent to press.

DISCLAIMER:

This book provides information about various types of rocks and where and how to find them. Before
entering any area in search of rocks, make sure that the area is open to the public or that you have secured
permission from the property owner to go there. Also, take care not to damage any property, and do not
remove any rocks from the area unless you have permission to do so.

Rock hunting in riverbeds, quarries, mines, and some of the other areas identified in this book can be
inherently risky. You should not engage in any of these activities without parental supervision. Also, you
should always wear proper safety equipment and know how to use any tools that you bring with you. You
should not engage in any activity that is beyond your ability or skill or comfort level. Failure to follow
these guidelines may result in damage to property or serious injury or death to you or others, and may
also result in substantial civil or criminal liability.

The publisher and the author shall not be liable for any damages allegedly arising from the information
in this book, and they specifically disclaim any liability from the use or application of any of the contents
of this book.

Printed and bound in the USA.   4882

CONTENTS

INTRODUCTION
STRIKING IT RICH? 4

CHAPTER 1
WHAT IS PYRITE? 6

CHAPTER 2
HOW PYRITE FORMS 12

CHAPTER 3
PYRITE TREASURE HUNT 18

CHAPTER 4
KEEPING THE SPARKLE 24

CHAPTER 5
BUILDING YOUR COLLECTION 28

GLOSSARY 30
READ MORE 31
INTERNET SITES 31
INDEX 32

Words in **bold** are in the glossary.

INTRODUCTION
STRIKING IT RICH?

Imagine that you're out for a walk in the countryside. You glance down at the ground. Something is glittering! Excited, you pick up a rock. It's made of many tiny cube shapes. The cubes are golden and shiny.

You think you've struck it rich! You start imagining all the things you can buy with this gold. But then you take a closer look. It isn't gold, after all. It's pyrite. This rock is often called fool's gold. You're not the first person to be fooled by it!

Even though it's not real gold, pyrite is still fun to find. Many people include it in their rock collections. Collecting rocks is a fun hobby. Why not build your own collection? You can start with pyrite!

Pyrite can look like gold
at first glance.

CHAPTER 1
WHAT IS PYRITE?

Pyrite is a type of **mineral**. Minerals are the substances that make up rocks. One rock might have a few minerals in it. Each mineral contains a different mix of **elements**. Pyrite is made up of the elements iron and sulfur.

Most minerals can form crystals. Crystals are solid substances with a regular pattern. They often have many flat surfaces. Crystals form when the tiny mineral **atoms** stack up. They form a repeating pattern of geometric shapes. Some crystals are very small. You need a microscope to see them. The crystals in pyrite are usually larger. You can easily see them. They are often shaped like cubes. Pyrite's shape and shininess make it stand out.

The crystals in pyrite often look jumbled together.

Many people have mistaken pyrite (pictured) for gold.

Fool's Gold

To many people, pyrite looks like gold. People have long been fooled by it. That's why it's known as fool's gold! Martin Frobisher was a British explorer in the 1500s. He found sparkly rocks when he explored what is now Canada. He sent a shipload back to England. But it turned out to be other minerals including pyrite, not gold.

Real gold is rare. It doesn't **tarnish** or **rust**. It is soft enough to be hammered into shapes. People can make coins or jewelry with it. For all these reasons, it is worth a lot of money. Why is pyrite worth less? Pyrite is very common. Over time, it will tarnish. It is hard but brittle. It will break if you try to hammer it into shape. Pyrite has a hardness of 6 to 6.5 out of 10 on the Mohs hardness scale. This scale tells how hard different minerals are, ordering them from softest to hardest.

FACT FILE

Name: pyrite
Chemical formula: FeS_2 (iron disulfide)
Color: brassy yellow
Mohs hardness: 6–6.5 out of 10
Shape: often cube-shaped crystals with flat, shiny sides
Strength: hard but brittle
Found: common worldwide in many different types of rocks, such as in **sedimentary rock** and alongside gold and oil deposits and coal beds

Using Pyrite

Pyrite isn't very valuable. But it's useful! Striking it on metal or stone makes sparks to light fires. In the 1500s, early guns used pyrite. It made sparks to light the **gunpowder**. Pyrite became a source of sulfur more than 1,000 years ago. This element was made into creams to treat skin problems such as acne. It was also used to dye cloth.

People make pyrite into jewelry. Its shiny faces, which are its flat sides, sparkle. Pyrite used in jewelry is often called marcasite. It was popular in the 1800s.

Pyrite has even more uses. It is an important part of some batteries. Scientists are looking at ways to use it to make **solar panels**.

FACT

Pyrite gets its name from a Greek word meaning "fire." It got this name because of its use in lighting fires.

Some people mount pyrite to wear as a necklace.

CHAPTER 2
HOW PYRITE FORMS

Pyrite can form in different ways. One of the most common ways starts when **volcanic rocks** wear away. These rocks contain iron. When they break down, tiny bits of iron flake off. They are washed into the ocean. They sink to the bottom. Dead plants and animals sink too. The layers pile up. Eventually, they turn into sedimentary rocks.

Now it's time for the secret ingredient: **bacteria**! There is sulfur in the dead animals and plants. Bacteria break down this matter. This releases the sulfur. Then the sulfur can bond with the iron particles in the rock. When the two combine, they form pyrite.

The sulfide-rich Rio Tinto in Spain runs through the Iberian Pyrite Belt. This region has a lot of pyrite.

FACT

Seashells often get buried in sedimentary rock. Over time, pyrite can replace their elements. This creates shiny fossils made of pyrite.

Pyrite can sometimes be found near oil deposits. People use pumping jacks to pump oil from the ground.

Pointing the Way

Pyrite is not the only mineral that forms in these conditions. Crude oil, which is used to make fuel, also forms this way. People who are looking for oil keep an eye out for pyrite too. Finding a lot of it may mean there is oil nearby.

Real gold can also be present in the same conditions as pyrite. Finding pyrite might even lead to a deposit of real gold.

Fantastic Find!

In 2021, scientists published a paper explaining that some pyrite has real gold in it. The pieces of gold are inside the pyrite crystals. They are very, very tiny. A human hair is 100,000 times wider!

Sometimes pyrite forms
a sunburst pattern.

In Water

Pyrite is one of several minerals that can form crystals in places with hot, mineral-rich water. These locations include hot springs and cracks on the ocean floor. Minerals in these conditions need temperature changes or chemical reactions for crystals to form.

Crystal Cubes

Iron and sulfur atoms join together in a cube shape. As more atoms are added, the crystal grows. But it keeps its cube shape. The cubes can be large or small. Some are 6 inches (15 centimeters) wide!

Pyrite can be other shapes too. Some crystals have eight faces. Others have 12. The faces often have lines or grooves on the surface. Pyrite sometimes forms in thin strands. They look like a porcupine's quills.

CHAPTER 3
PYRITE TREASURE HUNT

Hunting for rocks is a popular hobby. People who do it are called **rock hounds**. It takes a bit of patience. But you can find some amazing rocks!

Pyrite is a very common mineral. It is found all over the world. It is in many different types of rocks. You can look online to learn about the rocks where you live. Rock hunting clubs might have advice about the best places to look.

If you're lucky, you might find a lump of pyrite on its own. It is more common to find pyrite crystals inside other rocks. Their cube shapes stick out. Try hunting for pyrite on a sunny day. Look out for sunlight glinting off the shiny, golden mineral.

It can take time to find pyrite among rocks.

FACT

Chalcopyrite looks a lot like pyrite. It is made of iron and sulfur, but it also has copper. Chalcopyrite is softer than pyrite.

Geology hammers are just one of many tools that can be helpful while rockhounding.

What to Bring

You don't need much to hunt for pyrite. A backpack or bucket is good for carrying your finds. You may want to bring a geology hammer too. And don't forget the basics! You'll need drinks and snacks. A first aid kit will help if you get a cut. A responsible adult should always come along.

Know the Rules

Where will you hunt for pyrite? If it's private land, you will need the owner's permission. If it's a state park, you might need a permit. Some places don't allow rock hunting at all. Check the rules before you go.

Safety is important when rock hunting. Work gloves and sturdy boots will help protect you from scrapes and cuts. Stay away from mines and caves. Avoid cliff edges and going into water. A compass or phone with GPS will help if you get lost.

Fantastic Find!

In 1965, Pedro Ansorena Garret was exploring the mountains of Spain. He found an area with many large pyrite crystals. He started a mine that is now famous for its large pyrite crystals. Some look like golden sculptures!

Once you know the differences, it's usually fairly easy to tell pyrite (left) from gold (right).

Gold or Pyrite?

You've found a shiny, golden rock, but you're not sure if it's pyrite. Could it be real gold? There are a few ways to tell. Gold is usually found as flakes or lumpy nuggets. But it sometimes forms crystals, a bit like pyrite. Here are some tips for telling the difference.

Look carefully at the surface. Is there any tarnish? Pyrite tarnishes, but gold does not. Are there fine parallel lines? Gold never has these. Not all pyrite does, either. So if the lines are missing, that doesn't necessarily mean it's gold.

Can your rock scratch a copper penny? If it can, it's not gold. Gold is too soft to scratch copper. Pyrite is harder than gold. Even a knife cannot scratch pyrite. Whatever your rock turns out to be, make notes about it, such as on a catalog card. This will help you keep track of what's in your collection!

SAMPLE CATALOG CARD

TYPE OF ROCK: quartz with pyrite crystals

WHEN FOUND: October 4, 2022

WHERE FOUND: in a rock pile on Croker Hill

COLOR: white rock with gold crystals

TEXTURE: crystals have sharp edges

SIZE: 8 x 6 cm

NOTES: The biggest crystal is 7 millimeters wide.

CHAPTER 4
KEEPING THE SPARKLE

Some kinds of rocks look dull at first. You can clean, sand, and polish them. Only then will they look their best. But pyrite is different. It's golden and shiny. Most pyrite already looks good when you find it!

But pyrite doesn't always stay shiny and beautiful. Over time, pyrite will tarnish. This happens when it is exposed to the air. The golden color becomes dull. It is hard to remove pyrite tarnish without damaging the rock.

In fact, pyrite is pretty unstable. Water and air can make iron rust. Pyrite contains iron, so it can rust too. Rusting makes it crack and crumble.

Pyrite crystals may be mixed in with other kinds of crystals.

Pyrite that is rusting and crumbling often has a bad smell.

What's Going On?

Rusting is a chemical reaction. Substances combine to form new ones. Iron in the pyrite combines with oxygen in humid air. They form iron oxide. This is rust.

There is sulfur in pyrite too. When the pyrite rusts, the sulfur turns into an acid and a gas. The reaction will go faster if there is a lot of moisture in the air.

Preventing Damage

You can't reverse rusting. Once pyrite starts to rust, there's not much you can do. But you can keep it from happening in the first place! Always keep pyrite as dry as you can. If you wash it, dry it very thoroughly. Always store pyrite somewhere dry. A plastic box with a tight-fitting lid is a good choice. It will keep out moisture from the air.

FACT

Rusting pyrite releases gases. The gases can damage other minerals. If your pyrite is rusting and crumbling, keep it away from the other rocks in your collection.

CHAPTER 5
BUILDING YOUR COLLECTION

A piece of pyrite is a great start for a rock collection. What other rocks would you like to collect? It's time to go rock hunting! You never know what you'll find. Once you have a good collection, you can put your rocks on display.

You can buy a display case or make one from cardboard. Keep any pyrite in a sealed container, even on display! Make a label for each rock. It should have the name of the rock and some key facts. Then you can show your family and friends!

Why not join a rock hunting club? You will meet other people with the same hobby. They might have useful tips for you. You could even go rock hunting together! If there is no club nearby, you could start your own.

There are many ways to display your collection!

GLOSSARY

atom (AT-uhm)—an element in its smallest form

bacterium (bak-TEER-ee-uhm)—a single-celled microscopic creature; more than one bacterium are bacteria

element (EL-uh-muhnt)—a substance that cannot be broken down into other substances

gunpowder (GUHN-pow-dur)—a powder that explodes when set on fire

mineral (MIN-ur-uhl)—a substance found in nature that is not made by a plant or animal

rock hound (ROK HAUND)—someone who looks for and collects rocks as a hobby

rust (RUHST)—to develop a flaky, reddish-brown substance as iron reacts with oxygen

sedimentary rock (sed-uh-MEN-tur-ee ROK)—rock that formed from layers of material like sand and dirt that were laid down and pressed together

solar panel (SOH-lur PAN-uhl)—a flat panel that turns sunlight into electricity

tarnish (TAR-nish)—to become dull and less shiny

volcanic rock (vahl-KAN-ik ROK)—rock that formed from lava that erupted out of a volcano

READ MORE

Lewis, Gary. *My Awesome Field Guide to Rocks & Minerals: Track and Identify Your Treasures.* Emeryville, CA: Rockridge Press, 2019.

Lynch, Dan R. *Rocks & Minerals Backyard Workbook.* Cambridge, MN: Adventure Publications, 2021.

Potenza, Alessandra. *All About Rocks: Discovering the World Beneath Your Feet.* New York: Children's Press, 2021.

INTERNET SITES

American Museum of Natural History: Start a Rock Collection
amnh.org/explore/ology/earth/start-a-rock-collection2

Montana Bureau of Mines & Geology: Mineral Information
mbmg.mtech.edu/kids/mineral-info.html

University of Waterloo: Minerals for Kids
uwaterloo.ca/earth-sciences-museum/node/209/iences
-museum/node/209

INDEX

bacteria, 12

clubs, 18, 28

collecting, 4, 23, 27, 28

crystals, 6, 9, 15, 17, 18, 21, 22, 23

formation, 6, 12, 15, 17

Frobisher, Martin, 8

Garret, Pedro Ansorena, 21

gold, 4, 8–9, 15, 22–23

iron, 6, 12, 17, 19, 24, 26

minerals, 6, 8–9, 15, 17, 18, 27

Mohs hardness, 9

rock hounds, 18

rust, 9, 24, 26–27

shapes, 4, 6, 9, 17, 18

sulfur, 6, 10, 12, 17, 19, 27

supplies, 20–21

tarnish, 9, 23, 24

uses, 10

ABOUT THE AUTHOR

Nancy Dickmann grew up reading encyclopedias for fun, and after many years working in children's publishing, she now has her dream job as a full-time author. She has had over 200 titles published so far, mainly on science topics, and finds that the best part of the job is researching and learning new things. One highlight was getting to interview a real astronaut to find out about using the toilet in space!

Editorial Credits
Editor: Marie Pearson; Designer: Joshua Olson; Production Specialists: Joshua Olson and Polly Fisher